THE '45 AND CULLODEN

July 1745 *to April* 1746

The When and Why Books

The aim of this series is to take a familiar event in history and examine the cause and effect so that it no longer stands isolated from its background. Each book is clearly written for the ten to fourteen year olds and is fully illustrated with line drawings, many in two colours.

1. 1066: THE YEAR OF THE THREE KINGS *by W. L. Warren*
2. LONDON IN PERIL: 1665–66 *by Edward Fox*
3. DESERT VICTORY *by Edward Fox*
4. TRAFALGAR *by Donald Macintyre*
5. GALLIPOLI *by John Williams*
6. THE FIELD OF WATERLOO *by Aubrey Feist*
7. THE BATTLE OF BRITAIN *by Edward Fox*
8. BATTLE OF THE ATLANTIC *by Donald Macintyre*
9. AGINCOURT *by Mary Cathcart Borer*
10. GUNPOWDER TREASON *by Henry Brinton and Patrick Moore*
11. THE BOER WAR *by Mary Cathcart Borer*
12. FLODDEN FIELD *by Kathleen Fidler*
13. THE SPANISH ARMADA *by John Hampden*
14. THE BATTLE OF JUTLAND *by Oliver Warner*
15. THE '45 AND CULLODEN *by Kathleen Fidler*

THE
'45 AND CULLODEN

JULY 1745 to APRIL 1746

KATHLEEN FIDLER

Illustrations by
F. R. Exell

LUTTERWORTH PRESS
GUILDFORD AND LONDON

First published 1973

TO
MICHAEL FOXELL
AS A TOKEN OF MY REGARD

ISBN 0 7188 1928 4

PRINTED IN GREAT BRITAIN
BY EBENEZER BAYLIS AND SON LIMITED
THE TRINITY PRESS, WORCESTER, AND LONDON

CONTENTS

	page
INTRODUCTION	7
PRINCE CHARLES EDWARD STUART	14
THE BATTLE OF PRESTONPANS	25
JACOBITE INVASION OF ENGLAND	31
THE BATTLE OF FALKIRK	40
THE ATTEMPTED NIGHT ATTACK	48
THE BATTLE OF CULLODEN	54
AFTER CULLODEN	70

INTRODUCTION

L EGEND and romance surround the name of Prince Charles Edward Stuart, "Bonnie Prince Charlie", who made a desperate bid to regain his grand-father's, James II's throne for the Stuarts in 1745. Prince Charles had charm and courage that won the hearts of the Highland clans who flocked to his banner.

James II (James VII of Scotland) had been forced to give up his throne because he was a Catholic and the British people feared he would make laws to force them to become Catholic too. James II fled to France, taking with him his wife and infant son, Prince James. William of Orange and his wife Mary became joint sovereigns in Great Britain and Ireland. James II died in exile in 1701.

After William and Mary died, Anne, the daughter of James II, became Queen in 1702. There were many people in Great Britain who would have liked to see Prince James Stuart, son of James II, on the throne instead. These people were called Jacobites from the Latin name Jacobus meaning James.

Since 1603 Scotland and England had been united under one monarch but they still had their separate Parliaments. The English were afraid that when Anne died Scotland would choose a different sovereign from England, possibly the exiled Prince James Stuart. Statesmen in both countries thought the only way to keep Scotland and England at peace was to have one Parliament with both English and Scottish members.

In 1707 a Treaty of Union was agreed. Scotland and England were to be one kingdom under one flag, the Union Jack, which bore the cross of the patron saints of both countries, St. George for England and St. Andrew for Scotland. The Scots and English were to pay equal taxation and were to have equal rights in trade. There was to be one united Parliament in London. If Queen Anne died without children, then Sophia of Hanover, the grand-daughter of James I, or her descendants were to reign over the United Kingdom and Ireland. In 1714 Queen Anne died.

The Act of Union was not popular in Scotland and the Jacobites there thought this was a chance to bring back the Stuart heir to the throne, Prince James. They began to arm themselves and to plot secretly. They found a leader in a Scottish nobleman, John, Earl of Mar. He raised the standard in Braemar and many Highlanders flocked to his banner.

Not all the Scots, by any means, wanted the Stuarts back. Scotland had long been a divided country. The clansmen of the Highlands were quite different from the Lowlanders who lived in the central plain and in the cities of Edinburgh and Glasgow. The folk of Scotland were divided in religion too. There were Catholics and Protestants, the latter being mainly Presbyterians. Religion even differed among the Highland clans, some, like the Macdonalds being Catholic and supporting the Jacobites, and some, like the Campbells, were Presbyterian. The powerful Duke of Argyll, head of the Campbell clan, supported the Government and the Elector of Hanover who

THE HOUSE OF STUART

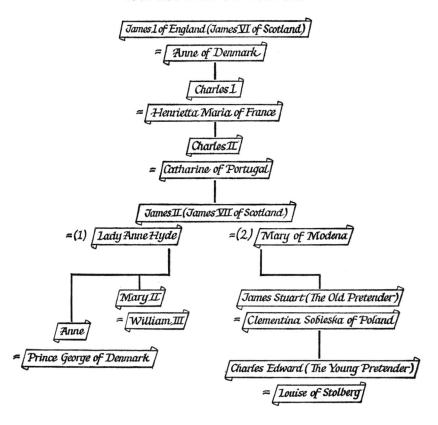

James Stuart's arrival in Scotland, where

became King George I in 1714. It is important to understand that Scotland was a much divided nation, both in religion and politics.

The Jacobite army marched on Perth and took the city in September 1715. Part of the army marched into England, hoping to gain recruits there. They were defeated at the battle of Preston. On the same day the Duke of Argyll fought the rest of the Jacobite army at Sheriffmuir. Night fell and neither side really won.

When James Stuart arrived in Scotland in January 1716 it

s greeted by the heads of some of the clans

was too late. The Jacobite army had dispersed. In the darkness he quietly sailed back to the continent and the 1715 rebellion was over.

The Government punished the rebels swiftly and surely. They were determined to stamp out rebellion among the Highland clans. An Act of Parliament ordered the rebels to give up their arms. To enforce this, General Wade was sent to the Highlands with a body of troops. The clans were also forbidden to use the Gaelic (Highland) language in their schools. Of course, it was impossible to forbid them to speak it

11

in their own homes. Though Gaelic was the language of the Highlands and western isles, it was *not* the general language of Scotland. In the cities and Lowlands English was spoken, although there were many Scottish words.

The clans were also forbidden to wear their tartan kilts woven in their clan patterns. Most of all they resented having to give up their fire-arms. They felt this left them open to attacks by powerful clans like the Campbells. In the past there had often been clashes between clan and clan, a kind of tribal warfare. It was part of each clansman's duty to march to battle at the bidding of his chief.

Inverness became linked to the rest of the Highlands by the new road system

A General Wade bridge

General Wade found great difficulty in transporting his soldiers quickly from one place to another in the Highlands because of the lack of roads. He urged the Government to construct roads to connect Fort George, Fort Augustus and Fort William and the towns of Crieff and Inverness. The work began in 1726 and took eleven years. Wade built bridges too. These roads helped the quicker movement of troops and opened the Highlands to trade too. A rhyme of that time says:

"Had ye seen these roads before they were made,
You would lift up your hands and bless General Wade."

PRINCE CHARLES EDWARD STUART

IN 1719 Prince James married Clementina Sobieska, a Polish princess. She was a girl of great charm and spirit and a devout Catholic as James was. In 1720 a son was born, Prince Charles Edward, later to be known as "The Young Chevalier" by the Jacobites and "The Young Pretender" (claimant) by the Hanoverians. He inherited his mother's charm and the hopes of the Jacobites began to centre round this young prince.

The Jacobites needed foreign help with money and armies to restore the Stuarts to the British throne. In 1743 a general war broke out in Europe concerning who should be ruler in Austria after the death of the Emperor, Charles VI. France and Britain found themselves on opposing sides. The Jacobites thought that this was an opportunity to make a bid to put James, the Old Pretender, on the British throne. James did not come to Britain himself. Instead it was decided that his son, Bonnie Prince Charlie, should make the attempt. Charles was twenty-three years old, handsome, tall, well-built, bold, and keen for glory in battle.

The French planned a large-scale attack on Britain in 1744. A force of 12,000 men was to be landed on the south coast of England and Charles was to go with them. A large fleet of warships left Brest. A strong British fleet appeared off the coast. The ebb tide prevented the British fleet from going in to the attack, but that night a fierce gale arose and many of the

Portrait of Prince Charles

French transports were sunk and the French fleet scattered. The remainder retired to Brest and the plan to invade England was at an end.

The French were not willing to fit out another fleet to help Charles to invade Britain. The Jacobites realized they could no longer rely on the French to support them with a large army. In vain Charles tried to persuade Louis XV, King of France, to give him troops. He was a determined adventurous youth and he declared that, failing an army, he would go alone. "I will go to Britain if I have only a single foot-soldier", he declared.

At that time Scotland was feeling galled by the taxation imposed by the Treaty of Union. In the Highlands, among the clans, there was great bitterness at having to give up their arms.

Seven prominent Jacobites had formed themselves into an association to bring back the Stuarts. They were the Duke of Perth, Lord John Drummond, Lord Lovat, Cameron of Lochiel, Sir John Campbell and the Earl of Traquair and his brother. They sent their agent, John Murray of Broughton, to Paris to see Charles. Charles told Murray how his thoughts turned with longing to Scotland. He said he meant to come to Scotland in 1745.

Murray was rather taken aback at this news. "Your Royal Highness should not count on more than four to five thousand men rallying to your cause", he told Charles, but Charles was determined to go to Scotland. The Jacobite Associators in Scotland were also somewhat dismayed at this news. Some of them considered it "a mad project" without the support of a French army.

Antony Walsh, a rich merchant of Nantes in France came to the help of Prince Charles with a frigate, the *Doutelle*, and another smaller ship the *Elizabeth*. He also lent the Prince £4,000 to buy arms and ammunition. On July 5, 1745, Charles sailed for Scotland with 1,600 muskets, 1,900 broadswords, 20 small cannon and a quantity of powder and shot. He wrote to his father, James, in Italy: "I am, thank God, in perfect health, but have been a little sea-sick, and expect to be more so." The adventure had begun.

One of Charles's ships, the *Elizabeth*, was attacked by a British man o' war and forced to put back to Brest with many wounded men. The *Doutelle* sailed on to Scotland.

On July 23 the ship reached Eriskay, a small island in the Outer Hebrides. There Charles sent for Macdonald of Boisdale whom he thought would support him. Boisdale, however, was luke-warm. He thought a rising would be "a bad project that could never be attended with success" and advised Charles to return to France. Charles replied, "I am come home, sir, and I will entertain no notion at all of returning to France for I am persuaded my faithful Highlanders will stand by me."

On July 27 Charles landed at Borradale on the coast of Arisaig. His arrival, with only a handful of French and Irish officers, dismayed the Scottish chiefs. They had expected a French army to come with him. Cameron of Lochiel, however, could not refuse an appeal to his loyalty. He came to Borradale. Even he reminded Charles that he had promised to come with a French army and Lochiel begged him to await a more favourable opportunity. The Prince answered, "I am determined to put all to the hazard. In a few days with the few friends I have, I will erect the royal standard and proclaim to the people of Britain that Charles Stuart is come to claim the throne of his ancestors, to win it or to perish in the attempt."

Cameron of Lochiel was won over to the Prince's adventure. This was one of the moments when the fate of the Prince's enterprise lay in the balance. If Lochiel had refused his support, then so would the other Highland chiefs and the spark of rebellion might have been stamped out. As it was, word went round the countryside and the clans began to muster.

On August 19, 1745, in the narrow valley of Glenfinnan, between high craggy mountains, Prince Charles raised the royal standard, in red, white and blue silk. There the Clanranald Macdonalds joined him, Lochiel with 700 Camerons, Macdonald of Keppoch with 300 men. Charles proclaimed his father as King James III of England and VIII of Scotland and himself as Prince Regent. Charles made a short speech and told the clans, "With your assistance and that of a just God, I do not doubt we shall bring this affair to a happy issue."

The Highlanders cheered him to the echo. So, in great spirits and confidence, Charles and his small army set off on their long march south. More clansmen flocked to his standard. Charles won his men's hearts by his willingness to share their hardships, eat their food and make his bed in the heather.

The news of Charles's advance reached the British Government. George I had died in 1727 and was succeeded by his son George II. His forces in Scotland numbered only about 3,000 men, many untried and ill-disciplined soldiers. The Government decided to send a small army under Sir John Cope to nip the rebellion in the bud. They assembled at Stirling. Large quantities of bread were baked for the troops to take with them and a butcher with a drove of black cattle went with them to supply them with meat.

All kinds of reports reached Cope: that French troops had landed: that Charles had a large army. No one seemed, however, to be quite sure where Charles was. On August 20 Cope set out from Stirling with not more than 1,400 infantry. He hoped that many of the Highland clans loyal to King George

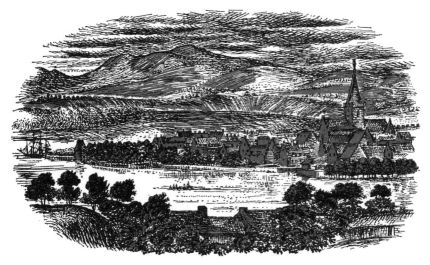

Perth was the first town which lay on Charles' route to Edinburgh

would join him. Few did. Many of them had Stuart sympathies; most of them waited to see which way the rebellion went before joining either side. Cope decided it was not wise to push on to Fort Augustus. Instead he changed his route and made for Inverness.

Spies brought this news to Charles. Now there was no army between the Jacobites and the Lowlands and Edinburgh itself. More Highlanders joined the Prince and he swiftly pressed on southward to Dunkeld and Perth. Charles, clad in kilt and tartan coat, riding on horseback at the head of his men, entered Perth. Here he proclaimed his father James as King and himself as Prince Regent. This was the first major city to surrender to him on his march south. He obtained money and supplies from the citizens. Here he was joined by the Duke of Perth and Lord George Murray, brother to the Duke of Atholl. Atholl was a divided house; the Duke was a Whig who supported George II; Lord George Murray was a faithful Jacobite. What was more, he was a clever general, experienced in warfare. Because of his Whig brother, the Prince regarded him with some suspicion, however, and Lord George did not get on with Murray of Broughton nor the Irish officers in the Prince's circle.

On September 11 the Highland army left Perth and two days later they crossed the Forth eight miles above Stirling. They had expected to be engaged by part of Cope's army, Gardiner's Dragoons, at Stirling, but Gardiner and his men had retreated to Falkirk. With the Highland army in hot pursuit, Gardiner moved to Linlithgow. He meant to defend

Linlithgow Bridge but before Charles's advancing arn Gardiner retreated towards Edinburgh. On September 15 the Jacobites took possession of Linlithgow quite peaceably. The Provost's (Mayor's) wife and daughters entertained the Prince, wearing tartan gowns and white cockades (the Jacobite emblem).

Charles continued his march towards Edinburgh and halted at Corstorphine, a village three miles south of the city. Gardiner's troops were halted at Coltbridge nearer Edinburgh on the south-west side.

There was panic and confusion in Edinburgh. Half the people wanted to defend the city: the other half was for letting Charles enter peaceably. General Guest, in command of Edinburgh Castle, was eighty-five years old; his second-in-command, General Preston, was eighty-six! All the same they closed the Castle gates and prepared to resist stubbornly. Not so Colonel Gardiner at Coltbridge. His men were weary, "their legs so swelled that they could not wear boots and overcome for want of sleep", so read Brigadier Fowkes' report. A Jacobite skirmishing party fired on them and Gardiner's Dragoons panicked and galloped off to Leith and later to Musselburgh, leaving Edinburgh unprotected. This retreat became known as "The Coltbridge Canter".

What was General Cope doing with *his* army all this time? He had marched from Inverness to Aberdeen and embarked his troops there to return to Edinburgh by sea. While Charles was at the city gates, Cope's army was still tossing on the waves. Charles sent a message to the Lord Provost (Mayor) and magistrates of Edinburgh demanding the surrender of the city. He gave them less than three hours to decide.

News reached Lord Provost Drummond that Cope's ships had been sighted off the coast near Dunbar. If only the Provost could hold off Charles long enough to give them time to land. . . . He sent another deputation to Charles to ask for more time to consider his demand. Charles firmly replied that unless the city was surrendered forthwith, he would attack at once. The city fathers could not afford to dally any longer. They summoned the citizens to a meeting and put the question "Shall we defend the city?" Most people preferred to surrender peaceably. A deputation met Murray of Broughton, the Prince's secretary, who told them the Prince only required the city gates to be opened to his army and all arms and ammunition to be handed over to him, when he would promise to make a peaceful entry. Once more the deputation asked for time, still hoping against hope that General Cope would come to the city's rescue. Charles curtly refused any further delay.

Charles ordered a detachment of the Cameron clan under Lochiel to enter the city. They followed close after the coach carrying the deputation back to the Netherbow Port (Gate) of Edinburgh. The gate was opened again to let the empty coach return to the stables outside the city wall. Lochiel and his men rushed inside, yelling hideously and brandishing their swords. The Guard took to their heels and the Camerons entered without a drop of blood being shed.

That same day Prince Charles entered Edinburgh in state. Cheering crowds lined the streets as he rode towards Holyrood

Charles received a great welcome from the crowd when he rode into Edinburgh

Palace. Charles was a handsome youth, tall, slender, fair complexioned with rosy cheeks and large brown eyes. His reddish hair was combed over the front of a light-coloured periwig. He wore a Stuart tartan short coat with red velvet breeches and a blue gold-trimmed sash over his shoulder. On his head he wore a blue "bonnet" with gold lace and a white cockade, the Jacobite badge. On his breast was the star of the order of St. Andrew and a silver hilted broadsword was girded to his waist. He was every inch "a bonnie Prince". That night and for a week afterwards Charles held state at Holyrood. Many ladies of Edinburgh attended the balls and receptions and were proud to kiss his hand.

On September 17, however, the gaiety came to an end. Cope had disembarked at Dunbar and camped at Haddington. Charles assembled his army again at Duddingston near Holyrood Palace. Drawing his sword he told them, "Gentlemen, I have flung away the scabbard. With God's assistance I don't doubt of making you a free and happy people. Mr. Cope shall not escape as he did in the Highlands." He marched on September 19 to meet General Cope and to fight his first pitched battle against Government troops.

THE BATTLE OF PRESTONPANS

THE strength of Prince Charles's army was still about 3,000 men. Very few of the cheering crowds in Edinburgh had enlisted with him. Their enthusiasm did not take them as far as that. Lord George Murray led the Jacobite army. General Cope's army was no larger than the Highland one, so the battle was likely to be even as to numbers. Between Dunbar and Edinburgh the land extended in a broad coastal plain, marshy in places. Nowadays it is drained and occupied by many famous golf-links. News came to Cope that the rebel army was approaching fast from Edinburgh and he took up a position on the flat ground near Prestonpans. With the infantry in the centre and the dragoons (cavalry) on each flank he awaited the Highlanders on his chosen ground.

Lord George Murray marched further inland to the slightly higher ground of Falside near Tranent. From here he looked down on the coastal plain and Cope's army. Between the two armies lay a belt of marshy land, full of ditches and difficult to cross.

When Cope was aware the Highlanders were on the higher ground threatening his left flank, he swung round, facing his army southwards with the sea at his back. By then darkness was falling. Cope placed pickets at the edge of the marsh, ordered fires to be lighted and his army settled down to get some sleep before day-break.

The Jacobites were more wakeful. Lord George Murray held a candle-light conference and proposed a daring plan. He advised they should march further east so as to come round to the left flank of Cope's army. A local Jacobite, Robert Anderson, knew a path through the marshes which would let the Highlanders come on Cope from the direction from which he least

Cope's Red-Coats met the full fury of the Highlanders

expected attack, from the east. Around 4.0 a.m., well before daylight, the rebel army was on the move. Led by the Macdonald clan they advanced through fields of stubble left from corn recently reaped. Their movements, silent as possible, were veiled by a thick mist as, guided by Anderson, they crossed the marsh. Dawn broke and the mist lifted showing the armies quite close to each other. Cope wheeled his army round to face the threatened attack and rode along the front of his line encouraging his men.

The sight of the Red-Coats roused the Highlanders to fury. They rushed upon Cope's army with a hideous shout. Cope's artillery fell back in disorder and were overrun by the charging Highlanders. The Government army was thrown into confusion. Colonel Gardiner was ordered to charge with his mounted dragoons against the rebels but, when attacked, most of his men turned tail and fled. Hamilton's cavalry was also seized with panic and galloped off. The unfortunate infantry unprotected, faced the full fury of the Highlanders' attack. The Highlanders hacked and stabbed their way among the terror-stricken Red-Coats. Cope did his best to rally his men but he could not get them to make a stand. The battle was over in ten minutes and became a rout, the Red-Coats fleeing. Among those who fell was Colonel Gardiner, commander of Gardiner's dragoons. There is a stone cairn erected to his memory at Prestonpans. Cope, with some officers and about 450 men retreated along a lane still known as "Johnnie Cope's Road". From here he took the road south by Lauder to Berwick. It is said he was the first general in Europe to bring the first tidings of his own defeat. The Jacobites sang a mocking ballad to celebrate Cope's rout.

"Hey, Johnnie Cope, are ye waukin' (waking) yet?
Or are your drums a-beating yet?"

It was a complete victory for the Jacobites. They had slain about 400 of Cope's troops, wounded over 500 and taken about 1,600 prisoners.

Prince Charles, with drawn sword, was with his army about fifty yards behind the main attack. By the time he came up with his officers, the enemy was already in rapid retreat. Fewer than thirty Jacobites had been killed. Charles wrote a letter to his father, Prince James:

"This morning I gained a signal victory with little or no loss. They have hardly saved any but a few dragoons, who by a most precipitous flight will, I believe, get into Berwick."

The next day Charles returned to Edinburgh but he ordered that there should be no public celebrations to mark his victory for he "was far from rejoicing at the death of any of his father's subjects, though never so much his enemies."

For nearly six weeks Charles remained in Edinburgh, hoping to build up the strength of his army. His numbers were very slow to increase. During October some French ships brought him some arms and equipment to Montrose and Stonehaven. Charles always hoped for French troops to arrive to support him, but these hopes were never fulfilled.

Meanwhile the Government was also busy re-organizing its army. About 6,000 Dutch troops were brought across the

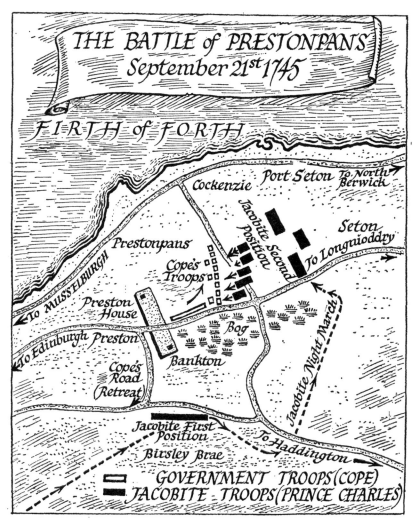

The Jacobite's night march gave them the advantage of surprise. The
result was a victory for Charles

North Sea. The English army was re-formed into three army groups: the first, including the Dutch, was commanded by Field-Marshal Wade and by the end of October was marching towards Newcastle; the second division was to go to Lancashire and the third one was to guard the south-east coast of England against a French invasion.

Against these forces the Jacobites had only 5,000 infantry and 500 horsemen. Few Lowlanders came to join Charles. Many of them feared the return of the Stuart kings would bring about the enforcement of the Roman Catholic religion. Though the Prince was a popular figure, there were great doubts about his success. On October 12 a Mrs. Hepburn of Edinburgh wrote to her friend, Miss Pringle. "His appearance seem to be cut out for enchanting his beholders. Poor man, I wish he may escape with his life. I've no notion he'll succeed."

Had Charles lingered too long in Edinburgh? Was this to be one of the causes of his failure later?

JACOBITE INVASION OF ENGLAND

B^Y October 29 Wade's army was at Newcastle. Charles wished to march against him there, hoping to rout the Government forces again. Lord George Murray and his advisers were against it and tried to persuade the Prince to remain in Scotland. Charles, however, was resolved on invading England, thinking that a great number of English Jacobites would join him. Lord George Murray proposed another plan: that the Jacobites should march into England by way of Cumberland and Carlisle, avoiding Newcastle. Accordingly, on November 3 the Highland army marched for England in two divisions: the first commanded by the Duke of Perth went by way of Peebles and Moffat; the second under the Prince and Lord George Murray, took a route through Lauder and Kelso. This was to make Field Marshal Wade think they were advancing to Newcastle. The trick was successful and Wade and his forces remained at Newcastle. Charles turned westward to Jedburgh and the two parts of his army joined again just north of Carlisle.

Charles called upon the city of Carlisle to surrender peaceably "to avoid the shedding of English blood" but the castle garrison fired their gun battery at the rebels. Thick fog hampered the defences and enabled the Highlanders to approach close to the city walls. They dug trenches around the city. The English garrison got word to Wade that the city was besieged but, though he moved his troops from Newcastle to Hexham, he could get no further for thick snow hindered any further progress.

The Carlisle garrison was composed of ill-trained soldiers. They mutinied and refused to defend the castle. The inhabitants, frightened at Charles's threat of fire and sword, begged Durand, the governor of the castle, to surrender. On November 15 Carlisle capitulated. Two days later, Prince Charles, riding a white horse, entered the city in triumph, with a hundred pipers playing their pipes before him. From this entry comes the song,

"Wi' a hundred pipers and a' and a'
Wi' a hundred pipers and a' and a',
We'll up and gie them a blaw a blaw,
Wi' a hundred pipers and a'."

There was an unhappy sequel to the surrender of Carlisle. Charles had sent the Duke of Perth and Murray of Broughton to arrange terms of surrender but he had not consulted his Commander-in-Chief, Lord George Murray. Unfortunately Charles had never liked Lord George, though he was loyal to the Prince. Lord George resigned his command but the chief officers of the army were full of dismay at this. They petitioned the Prince to desire Lord George "to take back his Commission". This the Prince was forced to do, for the whole army wanted Lord George as Commander.

A Council of War was held at Carlisle. Nearly 1,000 men had deserted from the Prince's army since the march began. Some officers wished to return to Scotland: some wished to wait at Carlisle till they saw what reinforcements they might

32

get from the English Jacobites: Charles was for going straight to London. Lord George Murray was consulted. He said that though he did not advise Charles to go much further into England "without more encouragement than he had hitherto received, if the Prince was resolved to march south, my small army will follow him". By his "small army" he meant the men of Atholl.

So, on November 21 the rebel army marched from Carlisle, leaving 100 men to garrison the castle. They went by way of Penrith and Shap Fell where "the roads were full of snow and ice" to Kendal. As it was Sunday they halted there for a day's rest. Then they marched through Lan-

Lord George Murray

C—C

caster, Preston and Wigan to Manchester. In every market-place they beat the drum for recruits but few men joined them. The Prince was an heroic leader. He marched at the head of his division, endured all their fatigues, was up by 4.0 a.m. and flung himself on his bed at 11.0 p.m. and "never threw off his clothes at night". No wonder his Highland soldiers idolized him!

At Manchester fewer than three hundred men joined the rebels. These were formed into the Manchester Regiment under the command of Francis Towneley. Though the Prince was delighted at this and talked about entering London on a white horse, his officers had hoped for 1,500 recruits. It was plain that Charles was not getting the Jacobite support they had expected. There was some discussion whether they should continue to advance. Lord George Murray suggested they should push on to Derby and consider the situation there.

Disturbing news reached them that the Duke of Cumberland was at Lichfield, waiting to block the Prince's advance on London. The Duke of Cumberland was a son of George II. He was a soldier with a good reputation, and with military experience. Lord George Murray divided his forces and by a clever feint he marched one body to Congleton as though the Jacobites were going to advance into Wales. This foxed Cumberland who marched to Stone to stop him, leaving the road open to Derby for the rest of the Prince's army. By the time they reached Derby on December 4 Lord George had re-joined them with his detachment.

An account of the Prince's entry into Derby is given in the *Scots Magazine* of that period.

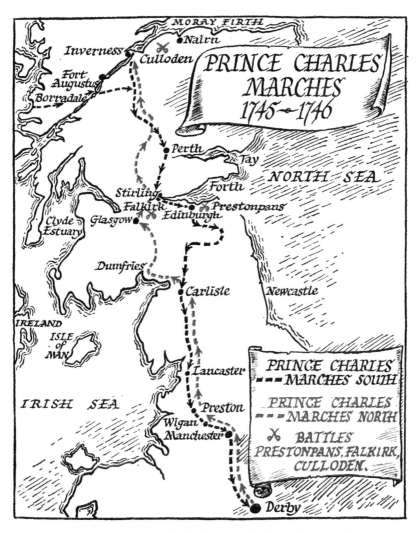

The route taken by Charles in his march to Derby and back to Scotland

"On Wednesday, 4th December, two of the rebel vanguard entered this town (Derby) and demanded billets for 9000 men. (This was bluff as the Prince had only about half that number.) They were followed by a vanguard of thirty men, clothed in blue, faced with red, in scarlet waistcoats with gold lace. They were drawn up in the Market Place. Bells were rung and bonfires made. About 3.0 p.m. Lord Elcho with the Life-Guards and many of their chiefs arrived on horseback. These made a fine show. Soon after, the main body marched into the town, six or eight abreast with eight standards, most of them white flags and a red cross, then bag-pipers playing as they marched along. They ordered that the Prince should be publicly proclaimed. The Prince did not arrive till dusk of evening. He walked on foot, attended by a great body of his men."

Next day the drum was beaten again to attract recruits. They were offered 5 shillings on joining and five guineas when they reached London. Only a small handful of men joined the ranks.

Though bells might be rung and bonfires lighted this was clearly as far as most English citizens were willing to go to support the Prince.

On December 5 Charles called his officers to a Council of War. He was in very good spirits and wanted to continue the march to London.

London was in a turmoil. It was "Black Friday" in the city. The shops closed. People rushed to draw their money out of the banks in case they had to flee from London in face of Charles's advancing army. It was even suggested to King George II that it might be wise for him to leave London. George refused to be disturbed. "Don't talk to me that stuff!" he told his advisers.

Though Charles was eager to press on to London, not so his staff officers! They took a very gloomy view. At the council Lord George Murray spoke first. He pointed out that though they had marched easily into England, few of the English had joined them. There was no news of a French army joining them. Cumberland was marching quickly to intercept them. He said: "If the people of London are against the Rising, then

George II

4,500 troops will not make a great figure in London. No less than 30,000 regular troops are converging upon us. In my opinion we should go back and join our friends in Scotland and live and die with them."

Other officers agreed with his opinion. The Prince declared angrily that he could not think of retreating after coming so far. He could not persuade the council to change their minds. At a second meeting it was decided to retreat to Scotland.

Utterly cast down Charles went to his own apartment and sat alone.

Who was right about this decision? Was Lord George Murray over-cautious? Might the bold march on London suggested by Charles have succeeded? To Charles it seemed that Murray always appeared to be holding him back. It is true many people in London were ready to welcome the Prince.

Most likely Charles would have had to fight a battle near London before he could enter the city. Four years later in Parliament William Pitt said: "The fate of England would have depended on the result of that battle." He thought if Charles had won a victory then that the people of London might have gone over to his side.

Be that as it may, Charles's Council of War decided to turn back at Derby. The turn-round of his army was the turning point in the fortunes of the Bonnie Prince.

The bewildered depressed Highland army returned the same way it had invaded England, through Manchester, Wigan, Preston, Shap Fell and Carlisle. Wade's army advanced through Yorkshire to try to intercept them. With the Hanoverians hot on their heels and with Lord George Murray fighting a sharp rearguard action they reached Carlisle. There Charles left a small garrison and they pressed on to Scotland.

The Highlanders forded the Esk river a hundred abreast, naked, with their clothes held high above their heads to keep them dry. When they reached the north bank they danced to reels played by the pipers to dry their bodies. Then, marching by way of Dumfries they reached Glasgow.

The prince stayed for a week in Glasgow to replenish his stores. He promised a peaceful occupation of the city if the citizens would supply him with £5,000, together with 6,000 short cloth coats, 12,000 linen shirts, 6,000 pairs of shoes and "blue bonnets". Grudgingly Glasgow provided them.

Meanwhile the Duke of Cumberland, son of George II, had re-taken Carlisle, and the Government army at Newcastle had reached Edinburgh. Charles left Glasgow for Stirling and besieged the castle there. The town surrendered but the castle held out.

General Hawley was in command of the Government forces in Edinburgh. He was keen to get to grips with Charles so he advanced to Falkirk. While his men were foraging for food there word was brought that the Highlanders had reached Falkirk Muir (Moor) to the west of the town. Bareheaded, Hawley sprang upon his horse, formed his dragoons into line and rode to seize the high ground on the moor before the Highlanders got there. As his army rode up one side of the hill, the Highlanders approached it from the other side. The clash had come.

THE BATTLE OF FALKIRK

IT was already 2.0 p.m. and dark storm clouds were massing in the west behind the rebel army. Hawley ordered three regiments of dragoons to seize the rising ground before the Jacobites could reach it. As the two sides reached the summit they came in sight of each other. The storm broke. The driving rain hit the backs of the Highlanders but lashed the faces of the Hanoverian troops and drenched their ammunition. Lord George Murray, on foot, led the Jacobite infantry. He gave orders they were not to fire till he discharged his musket. The English cavalry came on "at full trot" in good order. Lord George waited till they were within ten yards before he gave the signal to fire. The Highlanders' volley crashed into the leading line. At that short range they could not miss. Riders and horses slumped to the ground. Those left riding wheeled about, throwing the following line into disorder. The left infantry wing was left unprotected by cavalry. All was confusion and into it the Macdonalds charged with their broadswords. Hawley's regiments at his centre and left wing broke and fled, pursued by yelling Highlanders. Even the pipers flung away their pipes and joined in the charge.

On Hawley's right wing his men were protected by a steep dip in the land, almost a ravine. Here the regiments stood firm and poured steady fire among the clansmen and began to press them back. By this time it was 4.0 p.m. and the January daylight failing rapidly. The rain fell in torrents. The Government troops could not see that they were gaining the advantage. At this crucial moment Prince Charles himself brought up an Irish regiment standing in reserve ranks. Instead of charging, Hawley's dragoons retired. With the infantry they retreated to Falkirk, leaving Prince Charles in possession of the field.

Lord George Murray pushed on to Falkirk after the Government troops, determined to do battle for the town so that his men might have some shelter in the bitter weather, saying he would "either lie in that town or in Paradise". Luckily he did not have to fight for possession of the town as the Government army had already retreated to Linlithgow. The Jacobites seized a great deal of baggage, small arms and ammunition and

The castle at Stirling

provisions. We are told Prince Charles ate the supper intended for General Hawley! So ended the battle later known as "The Rout of Falkirk".

The Jacobite losses were small, about 50 men killed, compared with the Government losses of at least 350 men killed and Hawley also lost many prisoners to the Jacobites. He wrote that night to the Duke of Cumberland:- "Sir, My heart is broke. We are quite beat today . . . We had enough to beat them for we had two thousand men more than they. But such scandalous cowardice I never saw before. Our second line of foot ran away without firing a shot. . . ."

The Government troops retired to Edinburgh. The Jacobite leaders could not decide whether to follow Hawley's army to Edinburgh or to continue the siege of Stirling Castle. The bold plan of carrying the attack to Edinburgh was abandoned for the more cautious one of taking Stirling Castle first. Once again fatal faltering hindered what might have been a turning point in favour of Prince Charles. The delay at Stirling gave Hawley time to reorganize his forces in Edinburgh, time for reinforcements to arrive from Newcastle and time for the Duke of Cumberland to reach Edinburgh and take over the command of the Government troops.

The Duke of Cumberland was twenty-five years old, four months younger than Prince Charles. In 1744 he had been made General of all George II's forces both in this country and abroad. He was a capable soldier and he had the great confidence of his men. He was rather stout with small eyes and he lacked the charming personality of Prince Charles. He had a

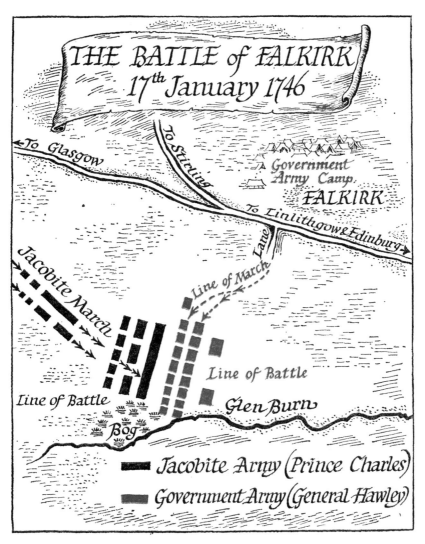

Another victory for Prince Charles

more brutal nature and waged war with a lack of humanity. Above all, he was determined to stamp out the Jacobite rising which threatened the safety of George II's throne.

Meanwhile Charles made little progress in taking Stirling Castle which stubbornly resisted his siege. Sitting down to a siege was never the clansman's way of battle and, bored by inaction, the Highlanders began to desert. Lord George Murray and the Council decided to abandon the siege and advised Charles to retire to the Highlands. When Charles received news of this decision in a letter from Murray and the Council he was so shocked that he banged his head against the wall and cried, "Have I lived to see this?" He replied, "I know I have an army that I cannot command any further than the chief officers please, and therefore if you are resolved upon it I must yield, but I take God to witness that it is with the greatest reluctance and that I wash my hands of the fatal consequences that I foresee".

The Duke of Cumberland wasted no time. By January 30 his advance troops were at Linlithgow. On February 1 Charles unwillingly commenced to withdraw his forces to the north. That very day they crossed the Forth by a ford. The clan regiments moved quickly. On February 2 they were at Crieff where a Council of War was held. It was decided to divide the army, the Prince leading one section by the Highland Road while Lord George Murray took the coast road through Montrose and Aberdeen to Inverness. The weather was terrible. John Daniel, a Jacobite recruit from Lancashire who wrote an account of his service with the rebels, said: "It blew,

44

snowed, hailed and froze to such a degree . . . that men were covered with icicles on their eyebrows and beards. An entire coldness seized their limbs; a severe contrary wind drove snow and cutting hail bitterly down upon our faces. It was impossible to see ten yards before us".

The two halves of the Jacobite army struggled through heavy snow and were re-united at Inverness on February 21. Two days earlier Charles had driven out Lord Loudoun and his garrison who took refuge in the Black Isle across the Moray Firth. At Inverness the Highland army remained for several weeks. During part of this time Prince Charles was seriously ill with a fever that was possibly pneumonia, but his army had several skirmishes with Lord Loudoun. The rebels took Fort Augustus at the southern end of Loch Ness, but they failed to take Fort William further west.

At this stage the Duke of Cumberland and his army followed the Jacobites at a more leisurely pace. They reached Aberdeen on February 27 and halted there for reinforcements to come by sea from Leith. Cumberland stayed for nearly six weeks in Aberdeen while Charles was at Inverness. Both sides were trying to strengthen their forces, Cumberland with more success than Charles whose Highlanders continued to desert, for their homes were close at hand. Also, for the first time, Charles had not enough money to pay his troops and he gave them an allowance of oatmeal instead. This was sullenly received. Probably both sides decided to let the bitter winter weather pass before moving again, as their men were quartered fairly comfortably in Inverness and Aberdeen respectively.

George II's son, the Duke of Cumberland

On April 8 Cumberland left Aberdeen with 10,000 men and artillery. Charles was still trying to collect his dispersed forces, some engaged in an unsuccessful pursuit of Loudoun in the Black Isle. The strength of his army was only about 5,000 men and he had very few cannon and trained artillery men. He had no money and food supplies were low.

Cumberland, marching by way of Elgin and Forres reached Nairn on April 14. Charles's army was mustered on Culloden Moor east of Inverness. The two armies were about twelve miles apart.

THE ATTEMPTED NIGHT ATTACK

LORD George Murray did not like the ground on Culloden
Moor. He thought it was too open for a battlefield and
would give an advantage to Cumberland's guns which could
sweep the Highland forces. Murray suggested the Highlanders
should move across the river Nairn to a more hilly position
with bogs that Cumberland's artillery and cavalry would find
difficult to cross; the type of ground that would suit the
mountain-trained Highlanders. The Irish leader, O'Sullivan,
was sent by Charles to view this position but he did not think it
suitable and preferred Culloden Moor. There was a clash of
opinions between Lord George Murray and O'Sullivan. Once
again the leaders of Charles's army were at odds. Murray and
his officers bitterly disliked the Irish and French officers who
surrounded Charles and to whose opinions he listened.

Charles was anxious to attack Cumberland without delay.
He suggested an attack on Cumberland's camp on the outskirts
of Nairn at dawn on the following day, April 16. Probably
Charles was hoping to repeat the surprise attack he had made
at Prestonpans. At first, Lord George Murray was doubtful
about it but the position regarding supplies was desperate.
Due to mismanagement no provisions had been brought up
from Inverness to Culloden. The officers in charge had
neglected to provide horses for the transport of bread and the
troops had only received an army biscuit apiece that day and

48

The Highlanders set forth on the night march

had nothing more to eat. Murray agreed to the plan of a night attack.

If the attack was to succeed it must be made under cover of darkness, so the march was timed to begin at 7.0 p.m. When they were on the point of setting out it was found that 2,000 men had gone in search of food! Some officers thought it would be wise to abandon the march but the Prince was resolved to launch the attack. Murray wrote later, "His Royal Highness continued bent on the thing and gave me orders to march." They set out at 8.0 p.m.

The night was very dark. The army moved in two columns, the first commanded by Lord George Murray, with the Prince and the Duke of Perth with the second column. Lord George planned to march along the north bank of the river Nairn till his column was within two miles of the enemy camp, then to re-cross the river to the south bank to avoid enemy outposts who might give the alarm, then to cross the river again further downstream to the north bank and take Cumberland's cavalry in the rear. The other detachment was to head straight for the camp and attack the infantry. The object was to catch Cumberland in a pincer movement.

The plan might have succeeded if an earlier start had been made and the troops could have been kept together. The moorland road was deep in mud, at places only passable in single file, because of bogs into which the horses sank. Progress was very slow indeed. Before the march had covered six miles Lord George was constantly receiving messages asking him to slow down to enable the second column to catch up with him. At

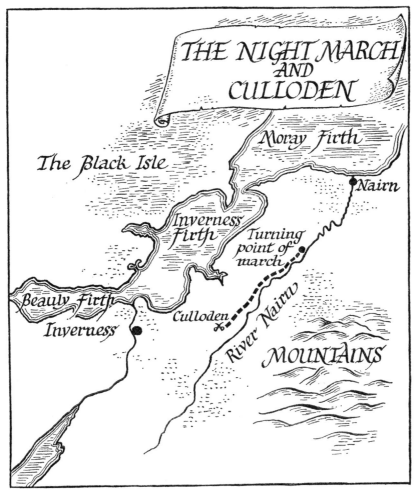

The route taken on the unsuccessful night march and the general area of the battlefield

one time there was a gap of half a mile between the two columns and the vanguard had to halt.

By 2.0 a.m. the Jacobite army was still four miles from Nairn. Many men were faint with hunger and had dropped out from the march. There was no hope of the two columns making a pincer movement at the same time on Cumberland's camp. Before they got there it would be daylight and all chance of a surprise would be gone. Lord George declared any attempt would "be perfect madness". O'Sullivan rode up with a message from the Prince urging him to continue the march, but Lord George and his officers had decided it would be folly to go on. Once more Murray's caution over-rode the Prince's bold plan.

Lord George ordered his men to turn about and take the road back to Culloden. Prince Charles, riding forward, met the returning men and was shocked and bewildered. He was for making Murray and his troops turn again but the Duke of Perth and Cameron of Lochiel told him firmly it was now near daylight and by now Cumberland would be prepared for any attack. Charles turned to the men about him, "There is no help for it. March back to Culloden." So, staggering with weariness, the Jacobite army returned over the weary miles to Culloden Moor, exhausted and footsore, hungry and cold.

The Jacobite officers did not realize that Cumberland would begin his march upon them as soon as sunrise. Some of Lord Elcho's rearguard, ready to drop from their horses, went into a barn to sleep. Barely two hours later they were wakened by the news that Cumberland's cavalry were in sight. They galloped to Culloden with the news. All was confusion as the clansmen, who had fallen to the ground in sleep, were wakened by pipers and drummers. The Prince himself had only an hour's rest at Culloden House. A meal of roast lamb was set before him but he refused it. "I can neither eat nor rest while my poor men are starving," he declared. He always shared his soldiers' hardships.

When the alarm was raised only 1,000 men were ready at first to take up positions. Charles went among Lochiel's regiment, encouraging and heartening his men. "Here they are coming, my lads! We'll soon be upon them. Don't forget Prestonpans nor Falkirk. Go on, my lads, and the day will be ours."

His army was drawn up on a far less favourable part of the moor than it had been on the previous day. Lord George Murray said he thought the ground most unsuitable for battle. There might have been time to cross the river Nairn to the hilly ground beyond, but the decision had been taken to fight on the bare flat stretch of Culloden Moor. The cold sleet beat into the faces of the weary famished soldiers as they took up their stand, shivering and sleepless, and awaited the coming of Cumberland's army.

THE BATTLE OF CULLODEN

THROUGH dismal weather of sleet and heavy rain the Government forces rolled on to Culloden. Cumberland had at least 9,000 troopers and cavalry against the Jacobite army of less than 5,000 men. Also he was well equipped with artillery compared with the few cannon the rebels possessed. By 11.0 a.m. Cumberland's drums were heard by the Jacobites and his men appeared over the horizon. The Government army could easily be seen for they wore wide-skirted scarlet coats over a long waistcoat and scarlet breeches with grey or white gaiters. On their heads were black three-cornered hats. The infantry carried long muskets and their white waist belts held a cartridge pouch and a bayonet. Each battalion carried two standards, the King's Colour and the Regimental Standard.

The clansmen had been waiting for them for five cold hours. On came the enemy "like a deep and sullen river" as John Daniel wrote later, silent save for the menacing drum beats.

The battle ground of Culloden lay between the Moray Firth and the valley of the Nairn river. It was a bleak countryside with the wind from the North Sea blowing over it. It supported one or two sheep-farms, the farms of Urchil, Leanach and Culwhiniac, divided by low stone walls. To the north-west of Culwhiniac was a large stone-walled enclosure. At right angles to this enclosure the Jacobite troops were drawn up on a slight rise in three lines. The Atholl Brigade (Lord George Murray's

Cumberland's soldiers poised for attack

men) held the place regarded most as an honour, the extreme right. The clan Macdonald had always claimed the right wing in a battle. Now that place had been given to the men of Atholl, possibly because they had the greater strength of numbers, but there was ill-feeling among the clans because of it.

A hundred yards behind the front line was the second line of support also guarding the flank of the first line near Culwhiniac.

There was a third line, the "Reserve" group, about the royal standard and Prince Charles.

Before his troops took up their final positions the Prince rode along the lines urging them to form up quickly. He wore a tartan coat and was mounted on a fine grey horse. The clansmen cheered him loudly. He took up a position beside his standard as the Highlanders made ready for battle. They flung aside their plaids to give freedom to their sword arms and hitched their kilts high, ready to charge. The pipers began to play martial music.

Cumberland's army was now within five hundred yards of the Jacobites. The Duke too rode along his lines encouraging his men. "My brave boys, your toil will soon be at an end. Stand your ground against the broadsword and target (shield). Parry the enemy in the manner you have been directed."

His soldiers had been trained to thrust their bayonets under the raised arm of the Highlander attacking a fellow soldier on each man's right. Thus each man protected the man to the right of him. The men cheered the duke and shouted, "We'll follow you, Billy!"

The Duke took up a position on the right of his orderly

drawn-up regiments also in three lines, but some of his dragoons were posted in the Leanach enclosure on the extreme left of his front line.

Cumberland had placed his artillery, ten three-pounder guns in pairs in the front line between each regiment. The guns were in command of Major Belford. There were some other three-pounder guns and mortars on a slight hillock to the rear. Cumberland's army waited in ominous silence.

The opening shots in the battle were fired by the Jacobite gunners from their cannon near the centre of the line. They aimed to the rear of Cumberland's front line where it was believed the Duke might be. One of the shots was a near-miss. Two minutes later the Duke of Cumberland's guns opened fire. Major Belford, in retaliation, ordered the shot to be fired at the group of horsemen round Prince Charles's standard. His gunners' aim was very good. A ball struck the ground in front of the Prince, spattering him with mud and injuring his horse, so he was obliged to take another. His groom, not far away, was killed by a shot which cut him in two. Captain Daniel, who carried the standard of the Prince's Life Guards, wrote in his account, "The battle being now begun, the whole fury of the enemy's artillery seemed to be directed against us in the rear, as if they had noticed where the Prince was. By the first cannon-shot his servant, scarcely thirty yards behind him, was killed." Only the urgent entreaties of those about him "seeing the imminent danger from the number of balls that fell about him" persuaded the Prince to retire to a less hot spot. Charles never lacked courage in battle.

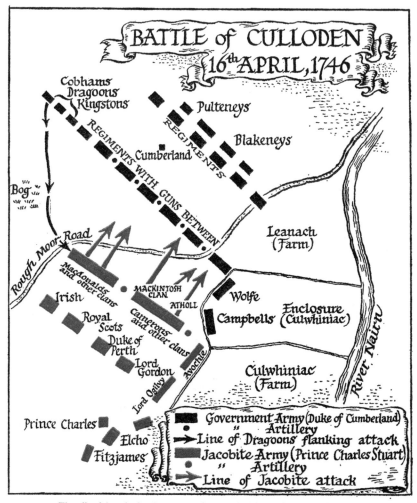

The final battle in the campaign ended in defeat for Charles

Cumberland's cannonade continued with rapid and accurate fire. His gunners had been well trained. The Jacobite gunners, on the other hand, were inexperienced scratch crews. Their aim was faulty, perhaps because they were firing downhill and their shot flew over the heads of the front lines of the Government troops altogether, killing only five or six men in the rear. When Belford began to concentrate his fire on the rebels' left-wing battery the Jacobite gunners fled! Cumberland's artillery was able to fire twenty shots to the rebel gunners' one. After nine minutes nothing more was heard from the Jacobite guns.

The clansmen stood with the wind and sleet blowing in their faces, blinded by the smoke from the guns, trying to close the gaps that Cumberland's round-shot was making in their ranks. They had been standing waiting for the order to charge when Major Belford ordered his gunners to load with grape-shot, a cluster of small iron bullets fired at the same moment, instead of larger cannon balls. The grape-shot fell among the rebel troops like hail, cutting great swathes in their ranks. The clans were desperate to charge from under this murderous fire but still no word of command came from the Prince telling them to advance.

Cumberland knew the Highlanders would break soon into a furious onslaught and he positioned his men to be ready for it. He ordered Pulteney's Regiment up from the reserve to the right of the line to meet the Macdonald clan facing them. He protected his left flank by sending Wolfe's regiment to stand at right angles to Barrell's, ready to give flanking fire on the

Jacobite advance when it should come. Behind the stone wall of Culwhiniac he also stationed the men of the Campbell clan. The Campbells were Whigs and loyal to King George and they served in Cumberland's army. They were old enemies of the Macdonalds and the Camerons and other Highland clans under the banner of Prince Charles. They were ordered to make a gap in the wall wide enough to take several horsemen riding abreast. They were to wait there, muskets and pistols ready, to take the rebels in the flank and rear when they advanced.

Still the Jacobite army waited for the Prince to give the command to charge! The Highlanders grew restive. They were sitting targets for Cumberland's guns. Lochiel, commander of the Camerons, pistol in one hand and sword in the other ready to charge, sent a message to Lord George Murray that his clan were "Galled by the enemy's cannon and turned so impatient they are like to break their ranks." Angry at the delay, Lord George sent an officer to Charles, urging that the order should be given to attack. Brigadier Stapleton also went to the Prince to tell him his troops, the Gordons, Ogilvys, the "Royals" and Irish could stand no more gunfire. They were in the second line. At last the Prince gave the order to charge.

Clan Chattan, the Mackintoshes, led the attack. Yelling with rage, their broadswords held high, they dashed upon Cumberland's Royal Scots and Cholmondeley's Regiment "like troops of hungry wolves", as a Royal Scot wrote in a letter next day. The attack was led by young Colonel Macgillivray of Dunmaglass striking right and left, leaping among the enemy. He died

of his wounds before the battle ended. Clan Chattan broke
through the first line of the enemy but not every man of the
Mackintoshes reached the Duke's army. Cumberland's infantry
obeyed their orders exactly. The men were three deep, the
first rank kneeling, the second stooping and the third standing,
all with their muskets to their shoulders. When the Highlanders
broke through the first line they were received by a deadly
unwavering fire. By the time the first line of the infantry had
fired, the second line took its place, then the third line took a

Muskets and bayonets at the ready—awaiting the signal to fire

The well-disciplined lines of Cumber

ry held the Scottish attack

pace to the right and fired while the first line was re-loading. This drill was repeated again and again. Edward Lunn of Price's regiment, wrote to his wife, "They came up very boldly and fast, all in a cloud together, sword in hand. They fired their pieces and flung them away but we gave them so warm a reception that we kept up a continuous close-fire upon them with our small arms, besides our cannon gave them a close-fire with grape-shot which galled them very much."

Hundreds of Clan Chattan were killed as they ran into the attack. Of their twenty-one officers only three remained alive. John Hossack of Inverness wrote: "Those of the clan who did not break the line were shot down where they stood and they slashed at the empty air with their swords."

The regiments of the MacLeans and the MacLachlans went down fighting too, stumbling over the dead. The Chisholm clan were shattered by the killing fire from the Royal Scots Fusiliers. "I never saw a field more thick with dead," wrote Edward Lunn.

On the right wing Lord George Murray's Atholl men and the Camerons swept down "like wild-cats" upon Barrell's and Munro's regiments, waving their glittering swords. Under the sheer weight of their numbers and the fury of the attack Barrell's regiment almost split in two, though they resisted obstinately. When Cumberland saw them hard-pressed, he moved up Bligh's and Sempill's regiments to support them. Barrell's men re-formed their lines with Sempill's and mounted their bayonets.

Murray's Atholl men were forced against the stone walls of

The battle raged in front of Culloden House

Culwhiniac and Leanach enclosures by the movement of the clans on their left. Behind the enclosure walls were the Campbells and part of Wolfe's regiment. They let loose a deadly fire on the flank and rear of the advancing Highlanders, though they also in the action killed some of their own side. The Jacobites were caught between two fires. Still they struggled on, climbing over the heaps of their own dead in fury and despair. Those who reached Cumberland's men perished on the enemy bayonets. The fierceness of the Jacobite attack slackened: they began to fall back in twos and threes, then in larger groups. They gave up the struggle against the murderous fire and the impossible odds.

On the Prince's left hand were the Macdonalds and other mixed clans. Their position was the furthest from Cumberland's army so they had six hundred yards to cross over wet heather and swampy ground under fire from the enemy muskets. They were slow in their attack till they were urged on by Macdonald of Keppoch, who rushed forward sword in hand. They found themselves faced by Pulteney's regiment who kept up a terrible running fire upon them. Three times the Macdonalds ran forward and halted to fire their muskets and pistols. They hoped by these three rushes to tempt Cumberland's infantry to charge them but the infantry stood firm and poured fire upon the Highlanders' ranks, shooting down the Macdonalds by scores. Then, on the Highlanders' extreme left appeared the horsemen of Kingston's regiment. The Macdonalds were likely to be out-flanked by them. On their right the Macdonalds could see the centre and right wing of the

Jacobite army giving way and moving backwards. In their turn the Macdonalds began to give ground too. The Jacobite forces began to break up.

Cumberland's cavalry commenced an encircling movement. Kingston's Horse bore left to chase the fleeing Macdonalds. The Dragoons came plunging after the retreating right wing. On the Jacobite side a few of the Irish Brigade, under cover of the boundary wall, tried in vain to halt the attack of Cumberland's cavalry. All was confusion. The retreat turned into a rout.

Prince Charles, seated on his horse, was utterly shocked to see his troops fleeing in disorder before the enemy. He had never dreamed that they could be beaten in battle. He begged them to turn and stand, shouting "Rally, in the name of God!"

FitzJames's and Lord Elcho's regiments near the Prince tried to form into a square, but O'Sullivan, the Irish commander, rode up in a panic crying, "All has gone to pot! You can be no help! Take the Prince off!" He was desperate with fear that the Prince might be taken by the enemy.

Sir Thomas Sheridan begged Charles, "Now all is lost, think of your safety."

Charles seemed as if he could not believe what was happening. He sat on his horse staring about him. For a moment it seemed as if he were about to gallop straight towards the enemy ranks and charge them himself but Major Kennedy seized his bridle and prevailed upon him to quit the field of battle. Elcho wrote later that the tears were streaming down the Prince's face. He could not bear to turn his back on the enemy but there was nothing else left to do but flee.

Lord George Murray had realized that the day was going against the Highlanders and he tried to bring up reinforcements. Through the smoke of the battlefield he led them towards the enemy but by this time the Jacobites were in retreat. For all that he formed up the Life Guards and Fitz-James's Horse and faced the enemy. Ten minutes went by before the dragoons ventured to attack them, then came the onslaught. Nevertheless the brave Jacobite stand enabled the men of Atholl to make an orderly retreat, though FitzJames's Horse protecting them suffered severe losses.

A mile away the Victorious Duke of Cumberland was cheered to the echo by his soldiers. He gave orders for Sempill's Regiment to march forward to take possession of Inverness. The cavalry were to pursue the rebels as fast as they could.

The Moor of Culloden was a grim place indeed. The heather was drenched in blood. The dead and the dying lay in heaps. Mangled men groaned for help. There was no help for them, only the cold steel of Hawley's dragoons who had been ordered to "mop up" the battlefield. No quarter was given. The wounded were shot and bayonetted where they lay. Few were spared. The Duke of Cumberland's orders were to show no mercy to a defeated foe. The cruel conduct of his troops towards the beaten enemy earned him the title of "The Butcher".

More than a thousand Jacobites had been killed in the battle and more than that number taken prisoner. Cumberland lost only about 300 men killed and wounded.

By nightfall the beaten remnants of the Jacobite army had fled in several directions. The right wing, commanded by Lord George Murray, made an orderly retreat across the river Nairn at the ford of Faillie and took the road for the south to Ruthven of Badenoch; the Irish and the handful of French troops retired to Inverness where they surrendered next day; the Macdonalds also fled towards Inverness where they were pursued by Kingston's Dragoons and cut down without mercy; the rest of the Jacobite army scattered in all directions. Prince Charles, too, crossed the Ford of Faillie with about sixty of FitzJames's Horse. Here he dismissed most of his men and with a few officers and Ned Burke as guide, he galloped away westward. He made a brief pause at Gortlick House and drank wine there with old Lord Lovat. From there he sent a message to Lord Murray thanking all his friends for their devotion and ending "Let every man seek his safety the best way he can."

The Prince then rode to the west hoping to reach the coast and find a ship to take him to France.

At Ruthven the last of the Jacobite army dispersed. Chevalier Johnstone wrote later in his *Memoirs of the Rebellion in Scotland* "We bade each other an eternal adieu. No one could tell whether the scaffold would not be his fate. The Highlanders gave vent to their grief in wild lamentations; the tears flowed down their cheeks when they thought that their country was now at the discretion of the Duke of Cumberland and on point of being plundered; whilst they and their children would be reduced to slavery and plunged without resource into a state of distress."

AFTER CULLODEN

THE Highlanders' forebodings did indeed come true. Cumberland was determined to stamp out once and for all the Stuart rebellion in Scotland and to put an end to the Jacobite threat to his father's throne. He ordered his men to seek out the rebels relentlessly. The Jacobites were dragged out from their hiding places after the battle and shot or clubbed to death. A barn where some wounded rebels had taken refuge was set on fire. When the wounded tried to get out they were driven back by bayonets into the flames. Even those who helped the wounded were killed, imprisoned or ill-treated. Bishop Forbes stated in *Barbarities after Culloden*: "In several parts of the Highlands the soldiers spared neither man, woman or child. They fell victims to rage and cruelty by the musket, the bloody bayonet, the devouring flame, famishing cold and hunger. The troops sported with cruelty. They marched through scenes of woe and marked their steps with blood." All this time the hunt was on for Prince Charles. The homes were burned of people suspected of sheltering him. Many of the folk were shot. A reward of £30,000 was offered to anyone who brought about the capture of the Prince. It is to the credit of Highland honour that no one betrayed Charles. All the time, the Prince, afoot with a few faithful followers, was dodging from one hiding place to another. He reached Borradale where he had landed the previous July, hoping to

Prince Charles' escape, with Flora Macdonald at his side

find a French ship there to take him away but the French ships could not approach the coast because of the English navy.

He found a boatman, Donald McLeod, who sailed him through a storm to the island of Benbecula. From here he sailed to Scalpa, off Harris. His presence became known, so for safety the Prince went to Stornoway on the island of Lewis. The inhabitants of Stornoway did not want him there for fear of reprisal from Cumberland. Though they would not betray him, neither would they help him. Once more the Prince took a boat and landed on South Uist. On this island he stayed for twenty-two days, living rough, but eating well of grouse, partridge and even deer that he shot himself.

Once again Charles had to move for safety. The hunt was up for him on every side. English ships patrolled the sea; Red-coats had landed on Barra; they were looking for him on Benbecula too; the Campbells were on Uist. Charles moved from place to place between North and South Uist. At last he had the good fortune to be helped by a lady of the island, Flora Macdonald. She obtained passes for herself, Neil MacEachain, a gentleman of South Uist and for her maidservant, Betty Burke, to go to the Isle of Skye to pay a visit to relations. The Prince was disguised as Betty Burke, dressed in a flowered linen gown and a white apron and wearing his own long hair. At 8.0 p.m. on June 28 they crossed a rough sea to Skye. There they were sheltered for a night by Macdonald of Kingsburgh. Next day they rode to Portree on the east coast of Skye where Kingsburgh had a boat waiting to take the Prince to Raasay, an island between Skye and the mainland. The Prince said farewell to Flora Macdonald. Because of the help she gave him she was later imprisoned on a troop ship, then in the Tower of London, but eventually set free.

The Prince feared he might be captured on Raasay. Once more he fled to the mainland and landed at Borradale. Though Cumberland's soldiers were scouring the mountain passes for him, he managed to make his way to Glenmoriston. For three weeks he lived in a cave, helped and guarded by seven men of Glenmoriston, themselves outlaws. On August 28 he joined a rebel chieftain, Cluny Macpherson, hiding in a little hut on the side of a mountain, a hut known as "Cluny's Cage".

All this time Charles shared the hardships of the faithful band of men who were hiding him. He never grumbled and refused to be down-hearted. Though the heather was his bed and he rarely slept for more than three or four hours, he was always cheerful. He took part in the hunting and foraging for food and even cooked it himself by a campfire. Small wonder that he won the hearts of the men who gladly served him and risked their own lives to protect him.

The Prince had good friends watching the coast for a French ship to rescue him. On September 15 the welcome news was brought to him that there were two French ships waiting for him in Loch-na-nuagh near Borradale. With Cluny, Cameron of Lochiel and many other Jacobites who came out of hiding when the word was passed round, they reached the coast. They were taken aboard the French privateer *L'Heureux*. On September 19, 1746, they sailed for France. Helped by fog they eluded the ships of the English navy on the look-out for them.

Portrait of Flora Macdonald

On October 10 Prince Charles landed at Roscoff in Brittany. The Jacobite struggle to regain the throne of Britain for the Stuarts was at an end.

Charles always hoped that Louis XV of France would help him to renew the struggle, but France's war with Britain soon drew to a close. Louis made it clear to Charles that he would give him no military help. Charles went to Madrid to try to enlist the help of the King of Spain but Ferdinand did not wish to be drawn into fighting for Charles either.

Charles did not forgive the French government for failing to help him with troops. He left France and for five years wandered about Europe before he finally settled down in Italy. There he married a young princess, Louise of Stolberg. He hoped there would be an heir to continue the Stuart claim to the throne of Britain but Louise had no children.

The Jacobites who had followed Prince Charles suffered severely. The scaffold was indeed the fate of many prisoners, especially the leaders. Altogether 120 were executed, some hung, some beheaded. Among them were the Earl of Derwentwater, the Earl of Kilmarnock, Lord Balmerino and Lord Lovat. A total of 684 men died in prison and on prison ships of wounds, ill-treatment and starvation; 936 were transported to America for life and sold as servants to merchants and plantation owners who wanted cheap labour. They were little better than slaves. The voyage in prison ships from Liverpool took nearly eight weeks and many died on the way.

The folk of the Highlands suffered terribly. Cumberland marched his army to Fort Augustus. From there he sent out companies every day to the glens, to pillage, burn houses and kill the inhabitants, if any had marched with the Prince. The chiefs were ordered to bring in their arms and surrender. Any man found with arms was put to death at once. Cumberland's men turned out women and children from their homes, plundered and then burned their houses. The wretched victims had nowhere to go among the harsh mountains, save to hide in woods and caves.

The clansmen lived by their herds of black cattle. These animals represented their wealth. The soldiers rounded up the herds and drove them to Fort Augustus. The land round the fort looked like a cattle fair. There they were sold to English and Lowland dealers and the Duke of Cumberland shared the money among his soldiers. The poor homeless Highlanders came to beg for oatmeal at Fort Augustus but Cumberland ordered that any soldier found giving or selling oatmeal to the Highlanders should be flogged with five hundred lashes.

Cumberland's determination to stamp out rebellion in the Highlands and to break the power of the clan chieftains was supported by laws in Parliament. No longer could the chieftain of a clan demand that his clansmen should march and fight with him. This prevented many feuds between quarrelling clans. It also meant, though, that the chieftains no longer needed so many men. There was much unemployment in the Highlands and many families had to emigrate to America to make a living.

The clansmen were forbidden to carry arms and to wear the tartan, the plaid and the kilt. Even playing the bagpipes, "instruments of war", was forbidden! Again the speaking of the Gaelic language was forbidden in public places and in schools, though, of course, it continued to be spoken within the homes.

What happened to the people who had been with Charles when he hid among the heather and in caves? O'Sullivan was with the Prince till they reached Boisdale. There the enemy was searching for Charles less than two miles away and it was decided the party must break up. Charles went away with two companions, MacEachain and O'Neil to seek the help of Flora Macdonald. O'Sullivan managed to find someone to shelter him till he could find some fishermen to take him to Ireland.

Flora Macdonald was taken as a prisoner to the Tower of London along with Macdonald of Kingsburgh. In June 1747 by the Act of Indemnity many rebels were pardoned and Flora was set free. She later married Kingsburgh and they emigrated to America. When the Civil War broke out, however, they returned to Skye for the rest of their lives.

After Lord George Murray had received the Prince's letter at Ruthven desiring that every man should seek his own safety he wrote to the Prince agreeing that "no hopes were left". He reached the east coast and got a ship for Holland. He reached Rome in 1747 and went to see Prince James Stuart, the Old Pretender, hoping that James would influence Charles to receive him. Charles was in Paris at the time.

Charles, however, was still bitter at the failure of his campaign. He had persuaded himself that the cause of it was Lord George Murray's over-caution and he even looked on Murray as a traitor. Despite a letter from James begging him to give Murray "a good reception", Charles refused to see him. Indeed, he requested him to leave Paris and Murray went sadly away.

When William Pitt came to power after 1746 as Paymaster of the Forces, he realized how unpopular the laws were against the wearing of the tartan and the kilt. He realized also the great fighting spirit of the clansmen. He raised Highland

Cumberland's troops pillaged and burnt houses throughout the Highlands

regiments for King George and allowed them to wear the kilt and plaid as their uniform. A dozen years after Culloden the Highlanders were fighting for George III against the French in Canada during the Seven Years' War.

Prince Charles never returned to Scotland. The Highlands were subdued and no sword was again raised in the Stuart cause. The Jacobites contented themselves with forming secret clubs and lifting their glasses to "The King across the water." For all that the "Bonnie Prince" was never forgotten. It has been said that it was *after* the '45 that Charles conquered Scotland through the hearts of the people. Romance and legend gathered about his name and he still lived in the love and loyalty of those who served him. To this day the Scots sing with feeling the haunting song,

> "Bonnie Charlie's noo awa'
> Safely o'er the friendly main,
> Mony a heart would break in twa
> Should he no' come back again.
> Will ye no' come back again?
> Will ye no' come back again?
> Better lo'ed ye canna be,
> Will ye no' come back again?"

The love and the loyalty his followers bore him is measured by the fact that not one of his poor half-starved Highlanders betrayed him when he was a fugitive, although there was a reward of £30,000 on his head.

79

Over Culloden Moor the cold north-easterly wind ruffles the grass upon the long green mounds that mark the burial place of the clansmen who fought for their Bonnie Prince. Over them broods an air of desolation and tragedy. There is a mourning silence. Over these sad green mounds that mark the place of the last battle fought on British soil, the Battle of Culloden, no birds seem to sing.